celebrating
Christmas

SHARE, REMEMBER, CHERISH

JIM McCANN, FOUNDER

celebrati⦿ns.com

**Andrews McMeel
Publishing, LLC**

Kansas City • Sydney • London

Andrews McMeel Publishing, LLC
an Andrews McMeel Universal company
1130 Walnut Street, Kansas City, Missouri 64106.

www.andrewsmcmeel.com

12 13 14 15 16 SMA 10 9 8 7 6 5 4 3 2 1

ISBN: 978-1-4494-2340-7

Library of Congress Control Number: 2012936746

Project manager and editor: Heidi Tyline King

Designed by Alexis Siroc

Produced by SMALLWOOD & STEWART, INC., NEW YORK CITY

Illustration credit information on page 70.

HOW TO MAKE A SNOWMAN
TOP HAT
SMALLEST SNOWBALL
CARROT NOSE
CHARCOAL MOUTH
TWIG ARMS
SCARF
CHARCOAL BUTTONS
HUGE SNOWBALL
CHARCOAL EYES
CORN COB PIPE
LARGE SNOWBALL
BROOM

introduction

I HAVE ALWAYS LOVED CHRISTMAS. Growing up, we would go to church on Christmas Eve, and then come home to a seafood dinner with our immediate family. Christmas Day was a different story. My mother would prepare a traditional dinner, and aunts, uncles, cousins, neighbors, friends, and anyone else who risked being alone for the holidays were invited. A motley arrangement of tables would stretch from room to room to room so that everyone had a place. You were out of luck if you needed to get up for something, but no one really wanted to. We'd sit for hours after dinner engaged in lively conversation. For my mother, it was heaven on earth. She loved a packed house that vibrated with the happy hum of people celebrating.

Life has a funny way of repeating itself. As the oldest of five, I'm lucky that my siblings live nearby, so now we carry on the tradition at my house. My wife, Marylou, spends the week before getting ready for the big day, and in addition to the forty or so loved ones who join us for dinner, we welcome many more who drop by. Like my mother, I love being in the mix of it all.

I grow nostalgic thinking about the common thread that ties the whole of my life together. Keeping the traditions of my boyhood connects my past and present—the people who shaped me with the people I have helped to shape. I truly miss the loved ones who are no longer with us physically, but when I sit down to Christmas dinner, their spirit is very much with me.

This year, after the last guests had left, I found myself feeling a bit melancholy. Our children are grown, and it is only natural that soon, they will want to stay home with their families

on Christmas Day. Plus, it's a long trip for the ones who travel from out of state.

"Who knows how many more years we'll do this," I wondered aloud.

"Enjoy what we have—don't worry about what we might not have," Marylou said. It was good counsel. No good comes from worrying about tomorrow. Instead, revel in the moment. There is no better time than the holidays to reach out and reconnect to the important people in your life. Share favorite memories, laugh together, and make sure they know how much you love them. In this season of giving, it costs very little to put a smile on someone's face, but when you do, it's the best gift of all.

one

deck the halls

I love parties, but even more, I love getting ready for parties. To deck my house for Christmas means that soon, it will be filled with family and friends. It means that soon, it will be filled with love. —CANDACE G.

Christmas is the season for kindling
the fire of hospitality in the hall,
the genial flame of charity in the heart.

—WASHINGTON IRVING

deck the halls

Each Christmas, my grandmother would hang chocolate coins wrapped in gold foil and netting on her live Christmas tree. There was one for each of her sixteen grandchildren, but also extras "just in case." With the illumination of the lights against the gold foil, her tree was one of the prettiest sights of Christmas. —PATTI M.

My mother baked lots of goodies for Christmas, but Daddy's favorite was coconut cake. When she finished icing the cake, she would let Daddy have a piece while it was still warm. That's why, on Christmas Day, the coconut cake, otherwise perfectly decorated, would always have a big slice missing!

—SHARON A.

Some of my friends can't wait to pull out their Christmas decorations, but to me, the best decorations are my three children—all home to celebrate the holidays. —NANCY K.

THE FIRST LIVE NATIVITY SCENE

WAS CONCEIVED BY FRANCIS OF ASSISI IN 1223.

WANTING TO BRING THE CHRISTMAS STORY TO LIFE,

HE BUILT AN ALTAR OF STONE ON WHICH TO PLACE THE

"CHRIST CHILD," AND INCLUDED TWO LIVE ANIMALS,

AN OX AND A DONKEY, IN THE SCENE. TODAY, THE NATIVITY

IS A HOLIDAY MAINSTAY.

Merry Christmas in Ten Languages

Mitho Makosi Kesikansi ❄ **Cree**

Boldog Karácsonyt ❄ **Hungarian**

Fröhliche Weihnachten ❄ German

Souksun Was Christmas ❄ Thai

Nadolig Llawen ❄ **Welsh**

Joyeux Noël ❄ French

Sung Tan Chuk Ha ❄ Korean

Feliz Navidad ❄ **Spanish**

Hyvää Joulua ❄ Finnish

God Jul ❄ **Swedish**

The **traditions** of Christmas are the best part of the **season** to me. My hands-down favorite is my parents' **annual over-the-top feast** on Christmas day that always, *always*, starts with **homemade sticky buns, bacon, and mimosas.**

As the day continues, **presents are opened, toys are played with,** but the dining room remains the center of activity. Guests change from year to year, along with **friends and family members** who are able to make it into town, and at times, it has been only the five of us in my family. Still, **more memories** are made sitting **around the dining room table** than anywhere else. —ERIN S.

deck the halls

Our big Christmas dinner is always held Christmas Eve, which means that there is not much happening around our house on the actual day. About ten years ago, someone came up with the idea of visiting New York City on Christmas Day. We jumped at the thought and an hour later, pulled into Penn Station. Our first destination was the discount ticket booth in Times Square for tickets to an evening Broadway show. We visited Rockefeller Center to see the tree and admired the decorated store windows along the way.

Since then, it has become our family tradition to spend the day in New York City, and we look forward to the holiday so much that Thanksgiving conversation centers around what show we should see. We can definitely say that we not only get great Christmas entertainment, but we are also able to add culture into a holiday already filled with love, family, and friends. —MARIA D.

THE ADVENT WREATH symbolizes the coming of Christ and marks the beginning of the Christian church's year. It is usually fashioned of evergreen, which represents everlasting life, while its shape signifies God, who has no beginning and end. There are four candles placed around the wreath, one for each period in the church's liturgical calendar. The fifth candle in the middle symbolizes the birth of Christ and is lit on Christmas Eve or Christmas Day.

✳

My
daughters
insisted on a live
Christmas tree, so
even though the one they
chose looked a little too tall,
we bought it and took it home.
My assumption was proved correct in
our living room—it was almost a foot taller
than the ceiling! Balancing on a chair,
I proceeded to cut the top off with a steak knife.
Even so, it still touched the ceiling, leaving no room for a
tree topper. It also left a permanent mark on the ceiling, but
how we enjoyed the year of the "too tall"
Christmas tree!

—SUZANNE Z.

Bûche de Noël isn't just a cake—

it's also the symbol of a legend. Centuries ago, a large log

was placed on the fire on Christmas night. If the fire went out,

bad luck would surely visit in the coming year. Likewise, all the

ashes from the log were scooped up and kept as good luck

against sickness, or to bring rain. Today, the Bûche de Noël is

a delicious French dessert of chocolate cake rolled with pastry

cream into the shape of a log.

My very favorite Christmas memory is when
I was nine. My sisters and I had piled into the
bed with our exchange student on Christmas
Eve to try and stay up all night to wait on Santa.
At 1:30 that morning, we heard a crash. She
tiptoed to the door, then suddenly turned and
dove underneath the covers.

"I saw an elf!" she screamed. Terrified, we laid
as still as we could, holding our breath and
hoping she wasn't seen or heard by the elf. The
next morning, there were pieces
of carrots and cookies scattered
everywhere—and of course,
presents for everyone! —LILY K.

Interested in visiting America's official
Christmas tree? Don't plan a trip to New York City's
Rockefeller Center, or even to the White House
in Washington, DC. The real tree is located in
King's Canyon National Park near Sanger, California.
A giant sequoia, the "Nation's Christmas Tree"
received its distinction in 1925. In 1956, it was
declared America's only living national shrine to
commemorate the men and women of the U.S. military.
It is 267 feet high, 40 feet across, and thought
to be around 2,000 years old.

ONE YEAR, MY DAUGHTER *wanted a Cabbage Patch doll for Christmas. They were in great demand, so I camped out at the local toy store in hopes of purchasing one. Although I was the first customer, I was told that the dolls had already "sold out." Hopeful, I filled out a form to be notified when they came in. There was no Cabbage Patch doll for Christmas that year, but nine months later, I finally received a postcard from the store notifying me that a shipment had arrived. My daughter had to wait the same length of time for her doll as she would have for a real baby!* —SUZANNE Z.

two

'tis better to give

'tis better to give

My mom is an incredible baker and her

Christmas butter cookies are highly coveted by

everyone in our family. Fortunately, every year

my Mom brings tins of cookies for everyone in the

family, but—still spoiling her oldest son after

all these years—she sneaks in one extra tin

especially for me to keep for later. It's my favorite

gift every year! —JOE P.

The circus-themed box for Barnum's
animal crackers was designed with
a string handle so it could be hung
on the Christmas tree.

*Over the years, my children have
questioned whether Santa Claus is real,
and each time they doubt,
I remind them, "If you don't believe,
you don't receive."*

—JUDY M.

'tis better to give

And going into the house they saw the child with Mary,

his mother, and they fell down and worshipped him.

Then, opening their treasures, they offered him gifts,

gold and frankincense and myrrh.

—MATTHEW 2:11

Having children has really driven home the idea that it is better to give than receive. Who would have ever guessed I could get so excited over flannel lobster-Santa pjs, *As Seen On TV* Eggies cooking cups, and a bicycle umbrella?! —CORRIE K.

It was Christmas morning, and upon hearing a knock at the door, my **darling little girls** Olivia and Lauren ran to open it. They had no idea they were in for *a big surprise* from Mommy and Daddy. There, on the front porch, sat the **most precious puppy**. "Texas" became their special friend and that Christmas morning became *a special memory* for Mommy and Daddy.

—YANIQUE W.

Happy, happy Christmas,

that can win us back to the delusions of our childish days;

that can recall to the old man the pleasures of his youth;

that can transport the sailor and the traveler,

thousands of miles away,

back to his own fire-side and his quiet home!

— CHARLES DICKENS

'tis better to give

In 1914, Charles Pajeau hired "elves" to play with his Tinkertoys® in the window of a Chicago department store. His creative merchandising was so successful that the next year, he sold a million of his Tinkertoys® sets.

The best present ever? Being completely
at peace, surrounded by loved ones in
a warm and happy home.

—RUBY K.

One year, my sister Sharon received
a bottle of Evening in Paris toilette water.
Instead of putting in on her wrists like perfume,
she flushed it down the toilet!

—SHARON A.

'tis better to give

We should give as we would receive, cheerfully, quickly, and without hesitation; for there is no grace in a benefit that sticks to the fingers.

—SENECA

The Old Fruitcake...

❋ People joke that fruitcake is the gift that keeps on giving because it is passed as a "gift" from one family to another. In ancient times, however, its longevity was a benefit: Its congealed consistency made it easy for warriors and hunters to carry it with them on long journeys.

❋ In the 17th century, fruitcake was restricted to special occasions because of its "sinfully rich" taste.

❋ In the 18th century, it was said that if you placed a slice of fruitcake under your pillow, you would dream of the person you were going to marry.

Y MOTHER loved the holidays. Every year when I was a kid, she would buy tons of presents and plan a big holiday celebration for our family. One year, while she was out shopping for toys, her car was broken into and all of the presents were stolen. She was devastated, and telling us that we might not have presents under the tree nearly broke her heart.

Flash forward to Christmas morning, when all of us were surprised to find shiny gift boxes and toys underneath the tree. Who could have done this? It still remains a family mystery, but we remain forever grateful for the Christmas Miracle. —ALISHA J.

The tradition of giving gifts is as old as Christmas itself. The first presents were given to Baby Jesus by the Magi. Later, the tradition continued with St. Nicholas, a bishop who was known for his generosity toward children and the poor. Legend has it that *Sinter Klaas* (St. Nicholas) brought gifts at Christmas, either through a window or down the chimney. This legend grew into the modern day Santa Claus.

three

the heart of the holiday

I WILL HONOR CHRISTMAS IN MY HEART, AND TRY TO KEEP IT ALL THE YEAR.

— CHARLES DICKENS

I have a large family. My dad is one of seven, my mom one of six, so Christmas Day is always exciting but chaotic. Ten years ago, to combat the craziness, my dad instituted a new Christmas Eve tradition that has become my favorite. On Christmas Eve after Mass, we drive into the city for dinner with just my dad, mom, sister, and husband. It is a quiet celebration over an amazing meal where we talk about the gifts we've been given this year—not those we are hoping to find under the tree.

Later, we look at Christmas lights on our way home, then trade our dress clothes for sweats before popping in *A Christmas Story*. It's the best mix of special celebration and quality family time there is. —MELISSA B.

In Nuremburg, Germany, the "gingerbread capital of the world," the *Christkindlmarkt* features the famous *lebkuchen*, considered to be the best gingerbread in the world.

Christmas is not a time or a season, but a state of mind. To cherish peace and goodwill, to be plenteous in mercy, is to have the real spirit of Christmas.

—CALVIN COOLIDGE

Love came down at Christmas;
Love all lovely, love divine;
Love was born at Christmas,
Stars and angels gave the sign.

—CHRISTINA ROSSETTI

Every year before Christmas my cousins and I get together with my grandmother to bake all of the cakes and pies for Christmas Eve. The best part, though, is not the baking. As we sift through my grandfather's old handwritten recipes, my grandmother tells us stories about how they grew up together. It's one of my favorite days of the year! —JACLYN F.

On Christmas Eve when I was growing up, we would go to my Aunt Mary's in the Bronx for a traditional Italian meal of seven fishes. She had a one-bedroom apartment, but we would fit over 50 people around one big table in her living room. Once you sat down, you did not get up. There was no easy way out of your chair, but no one cared. The delicious food, great conversation and warmth from love and family kept you glued to your seat.

Now, Aunt Mary has been gone for 15 years, and while we still celebrate with the same meal in the comfort of a formal dining room, I would give anything to be back at the big table in that little room. —LISA H.

the heart of the holiday

On December 13, one of the darkest days of the year, Sweden celebrates St. Lucia Day, or the Festival of Lights, to symbolize the promise of the sun's return. Lucia was a young girl from the fourth century who, according to legend, was blinded for her Christian beliefs. As such, she is the patron saint of the blind.

Historically on this day, a young girl dressed in white with a red sash around her waist and a wreath of lit candles on her head would carry baked goods to neighbors. Today, the tradition continues, with the oldest girl in each family given the honor of representing St. Lucia.

y husband passed away at age 49, leaving me with two sons. The first Christmas without him, I wanted to do something special—I couldn't bear to stay in town. One of our favorite places to visit had always been Gatlinburg, Tennessee, so I bought a two-foot decorated Christmas tree, packed my silver candelabra, red candles, and white tablecloth, and headed for the mountains. When we arrived, I decorated our motel room, trying to make the best of the situation. We went shopping and visited relatives who lived close by. Looking back, we had a great time despite our profound sadness over losing a husband and father. The three of us will forever remember that Christmas as a new beginning. —MILLIE G.

the heart of the holiday

The music for "O Holy Night," written by French composer Adolphe-Charles Adam, has become a beloved holiday carol, but in 1847, church officials denounced the song for its "lack of musical taste and total absence of the spirit of religion." It was a low blow for Adam, who also wrote the ballet *Giselle*.

Every year after all the gifts have been opened,
we each grab our favorites and head to the
front porch for a group picture. We're usually
in pjs and sweats, with uncombed hair
and sleepy eyes. Natural, completely at ease,
and a bit quirky—as our family is—it's my
favorite souvenir of Christmas.

—JUDY M.

CHRISTMAS IS THE ONLY MORNING OF THE YEAR WHEN WE MOTHERS DON'T COMPLAIN ABOUT CHILDREN STREWING PAPER FROM ONE CORNER OF THE LIVING ROOM TO THE OTHER. MAYBE THERE IS A LESSON IN ALL THAT MADNESS — TO SLOW DOWN, ENJOY THE MOMENT, AND REALIZE THAT A LITTLE CRAZINESS DOESN'T HURT ANYTHING AND MESSES DO GET CLEANED UP. —CHRISTINA C.

It never fails. Santa always does a drive-by on Christmas Eve, dropping a sack of pajamas onto our lawn for the family. How does he know that we are always in need of new pajamas? It's part of the mystery of the season.

—BILL S.

Poinsettias, "Flower of the Holy Night," were brought from Mexico to the United States by Joel Poinsett in 1829. In their native country, they grow as shrubs and can reach ten feet in height.

Legend has it that on Christmas Eve long ago, a poor boy went to church, saddened that he had no gift to bring the Holy Child. Crying as he knelt on the ground outside, he prayed for forgiveness, assuring God that he loved him even though he had no gift. When he finished and got up, a green plant with gorgeous blooms of red sprung from the ground.

Every year after Thanksgiving, my Mom and I would spend the entire day decorating for Christmas. When the house was decked top to bottom, we would cuddle on the couch with hot chocolate and cookies to watch *The Muppets' Christmas Carol*.

Mom passed away six years ago, but I still continue the tradition with friends. And even though I am now 30 years old, nothing makes me feel as much like a child-at-heart as Christmas! —LUCY KATE R.

four

Christmas blessings

The Christmas that matters most

to me was the Christmas of 1996. I was living in the family
shelter with my mom and three young siblings. Even though
Mom was very sick, she had tried so hard to find the right home
for us so we would have a safe place to live. I asked Santa for the
one thing that mattered most to my family: a place to call home.
Two days before Christmas, and after months of living in the
homeless shelter, we moved into our HOME, a blessing my mom
worked so hard for and one that Santa helped to give our family.
Now, the holidays are a reminder to us of what we endured
and the blessings and joy our family has been given: the safety
and comfort of family, the warmth of a home, and the blessing
of good health. —AMIRA A.

Christmas blessings

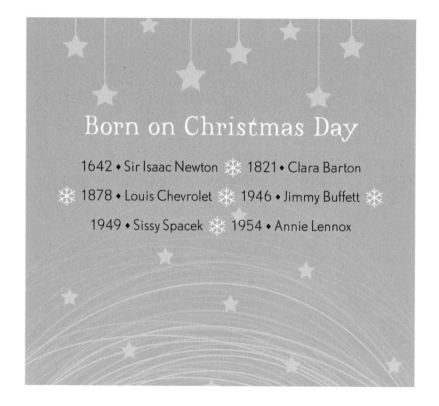

Born on Christmas Day

1642 ◆ Sir Isaac Newton ❄ 1821 ◆ Clara Barton

❄ 1878 ◆ Louis Chevrolet ❄ 1946 ◆ Jimmy Buffett ❄

1949 ◆ Sissy Spacek ❄ 1954 ◆ Annie Lennox

Before Christmas dinner, we always go around the table, with each person naming a blessing from the past year. It's a good way to remember why we celebrate the season. —HELEN T.

*a*t the beginning of Christmas Mass every year, the little ones choose stuffed animals to add to the manger scene before presenting the Christmas Pageant. One year, at the end of Mass, the Priest was processing out of church when my son Mitchell, who played a shepherd in the play, reached out and grabbed him by his vestments. Father Tom, who is easily 6'2", bent low so the three-year-old could whisper into his ear. He nodded, and Mitchell ran to the alter and grabbed his pink pig from the mound of animals. He then threw the pig into the air with great glee, making a perfect catch as he descended the stairs. The church erupted with laughter and applause. Clearly, it had been a long hour without pig in his arms. It was also a perfect reminder in the Christmas season of our Father's love for us. —ALICE W.

*Perhaps the best Yuletide decoration
is being wreathed in smiles.*

—ANON

*At Christmas play and
make good cheer,
For Christmas comes but once a year.*

—THOMAS TUSSER

Silent night! Holy night!

All is calm, all is bright,

Round yon virgin mother and Child

Holy Infant so tender and mild;

Sleep in heavenly peace,

Sleep in heavenly peace.

— JOSEPH MOHR

Christmas blessings

Our family tradition of serving dinner at the local homeless shelter on *Christmas Eve* started when our oldest daughter was seven. We dressed up, reviewed proper "serving etiquette," and made a big deal of what a privilege it is to be able to serve others in this way. Six years later, it has become our family's favorite night of the year—and finally, after a long wait, our youngest, now seven, got her chance to join us! —HEIDI K.

"Yes, Virginia,
there is a
Santa Claus.
He exists as certainly
as love and generosity and
devotion exist, and you know
that they abound and give to your life
its highest beauty and joy.
Alas! how dreary would be the world
if there were no Santa Claus."

—FRANCIS PHARCELLUS CHURCH

AST CHRISTMAS WAS BITTERSWEET. We had lost my mom in March, and I was not looking forward to our first holiday without her. Shortly after her death, however, my daughter found out she was pregnant. She was due the second week of January. As luck would have it, she went into labor early Christmas morning and had my granddaughter that afternoon. I like to think that the two angels met in heaven before the newest one came down to join us! —BARBARA K.

*The ornaments on our tree
are an assemblage of memories~
each a Christmas blessing.*

—VELMA L.

I have always thought of Christmas time,

when it has come round,

as a good time;

a kind, forgiving, charitable time;

the only time I know of,

in the long calendar of the year,

when men and women seem by one consent

to open their shut-up hearts freely,

and to think of people below them as

if they really were fellow passengers to the grave,

and not another race of creatures bound on other journeys.

—CHARLES DICKENS

I t was a very cold Christmas, and because our refrigerator was stuffed, I decided to put the turkey and ham in a cooler in the garage. The next morning, I went to get the ham— but the cooler was empty. I asked everyone: *Have you seen the ham?* No luck. Only when we started to think back did we realize that I had taken the ham out of the cooler and set it on the work bench, walking away for only a minute to get the turkey.

So . . . in the two minutes it took me to walk inside, Jake and Bronco, our yellow labs, had snatched it and ran to the backyard, past our oblivious guys playing ball, and proceeded to eat the entire ham, bone and all. The only evidence left was the netting.

Thank goodness our good friend, Erv, called as always on his way over to see if we needed anything. Obviously, we said a HAM! —RACHEL S.

Joy to the world! The Lord is come;
Let earth receive her King;
Let every heart prepare him room,
And heaven and nature sing,
And heaven and nature sing,
And heaven, and heaven, and nature sing.

—ISAAC WATTS

illustration credits